WOODLAND WILDLIFE

Gray Squirrels

by G. G. Lake

CAPSTONE PRESS
a capstone imprint

Pebble®
Plus

Pebble Plus is published by Capstone Press,
1710 Roe Crest Drive, North Mankato, Minnesota 56003
www.mycapstone.com

Library of Congress Cataloging-in-Publication Data
Names: Lake, G. G., author.
Title: Gray squirrels / by G. G. Lake.
Description: North Mankato, Minnesota : Capstone Press, [2017] | Series:
  Pebble plus. Woodland wildlife | Audience: Ages 4–8. | Audience: K to
  grade 3. | Includes bibliographical references and index.
Identifiers: LCCN 2016001919| ISBN 9781515708186 (library binding) | ISBN
  9781515708254 (pbk.) | ISBN 9781515708315 (ebook (pdf))
Subjects: LCSH: Gray squirrel—Juvenile literature.
Classification: LCC QL737.R68 L345 2017 | DDC 599.36/2—dc23
LC record available at http://lccn.loc.gov/2016001919

Editorial Credits
Gena Chester, editor; Juliette Peters, designer; Wanda Winch, media researcher;
Steve Walker, production specialist

Photo Credits
Alamy: FLPA, 11; Minden Pictures: Stephen Dalton, 5; Shutterstock: alicedaniel,
illustrated forest items, Anna Subbotina, 22–23, AR Pictures, tree bark design, Bob
Orsillo, 7, Dom1530, 21, elina, 24, Emi, 9 (top), gdvcom, 13, Heiko Kiera, 15, lightpoet, 19,
Maciej Olszewski, cover, mythja, 1, P.Preeda, 17, Stawek, 9 (map), Sunny Forest, 3

Note to Parents and Teachers

The Woodland Wildlife set supports national curriculum standards for science related
to life science. This book describes and illustrates gray squirrels. The images support
early readers in understanding the text. The repetition of words and phrases
helps early readers learn new words. This book also introduces early readers to
subject-specific vocabulary words, which are defined in the Glossary section. Early
readers may need assistance to read some words and to use the Table of Contents,
Glossary, Read More, Internet Sites, Critical Thinking Using the Common Core,
and Index sections of the book.

Table of Contents

Tree Jumpers

A small rodent hops from tree to tree. Its long, bushy tail keeps it balanced. This tree jumper is a gray squirrel!

Gray squirrels have gray or black fur. Parts of their coats can be brown. Sometimes their bellies are white.

Gray squirrels are found
in North America and
in Europe. In both places,
they live in the woods.

Gray Squirrel Range Map

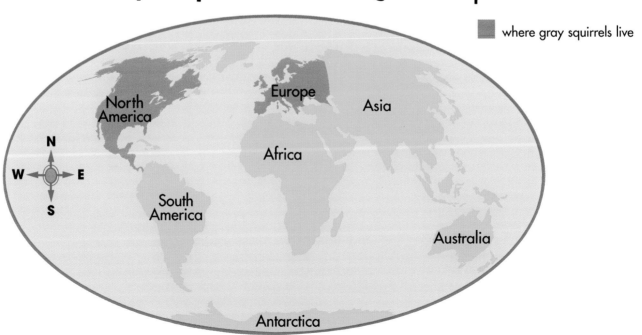

where gray squirrels live

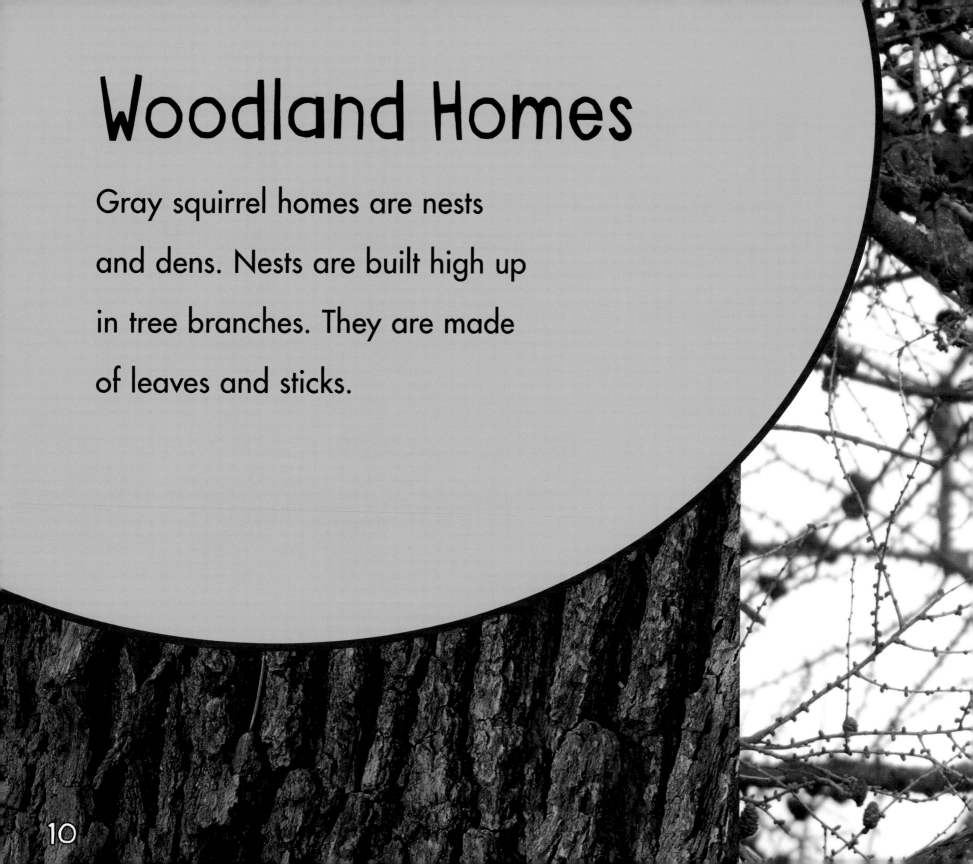

Woodland Homes

Gray squirrel homes are nests and dens. Nests are built high up in tree branches. They are made of leaves and sticks.

Squirrels live in dens in winter.

Dens are found in hollow trees.

There squirrels stay warm

in the cold weather.

Forest Food

Gray squirrels eat nuts, flowers, and tree bark. They bury some of their food in the ground. Squirrels eat this food in winter.

Staying Safe

Squirrels have a lot of predators. Hawks, owls, raccoons, and foxes hunt them. Gray squirrels stay close to their homes to stay safe.

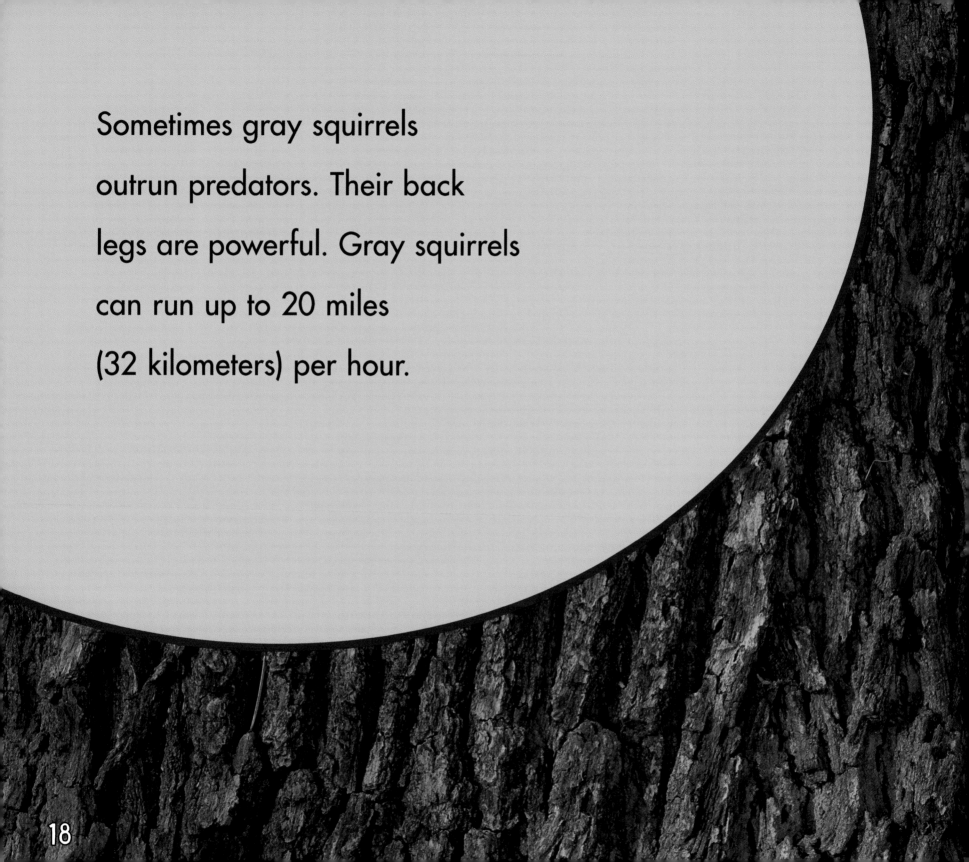

Sometimes gray squirrels
outrun predators. Their back
legs are powerful. Gray squirrels
can run up to 20 miles
(32 kilometers) per hour.

Baby Squirrels

Mother squirrels have two to eight babies twice a year. Babies stay with their mothers for two to three months. Then the young squirrels are ready to leave the nest.

Glossary

balance—to keep steady and not fall over

bark—the hard covering of a tree

den—a trunk of a tree where wild animals may live

fur—thick hair that covers an animal

hollow—empty on the inside

hunt—to find and catch animals for food

nest—the home of insects, birds, or animals

predator—an animal that hunts other animals for food

rodent—a mammal with long front teeth used for gnawing; rats, mice, and squirrels are rodents

woods—a large area covered with trees and plants; forests are sometimes called woods

Read More

Leaf, Christina. *Gray Squirrels.* Minneapolis: Bellwether Media, 2015.

Murray, Julie. *Squirrels.* Everyday Animals. Minneapolis: Abdo Kids, 2016.

Schuh, Mari. *Squirrels.* North Mankato, Minn.: Capstone Press, 2015.

Internet Sites

FactHound offers a safe, fun way to find Internet sites related to this book. All of the sites on FactHound have been researched by our staff.

Here's all you do:

Visit *www.facthound.com*

Type in this code: 9781515708186

Super-cool stuff!

Check out projects, games and lots more at
www.capstonekids.com

Critical Thinking Using the Common Core

1. What does the word hollow mean? (Craft and Structure)

2. How long do baby squirrels stay with their mother? (Key Ideas and Details)

3. Where in the world do gray squirrels live? (Key Ideas and Details)

Index